The
New Supervisor's COACH

A Guide to the Top 3 Priorities in Your New Position

Dennis Wade

Tyler Wade

Published by Broadstone Publishing.

broadstonepublishing.com

ISBN: 978-0-615-39341-4 (pbk.)

Printed in the United States of America

Table of Contents

Preface

It's no secret that too many employees are promoted to supervisory or management positions with little or no formal training. You are told that the "boot camp" or academy for new supervisors won't be offered again for nine months. Unfortunately, your boss is entering the busiest time of the year and won't be available except for a few minutes here or there to help you "put out fires." The only good news is that you can blunder your way through the first few months without getting into too much trouble because you "don't know better" or because you "haven't received training yet."

That's easy for them to say. The truth is that you want to begin your career in management the best way possible. You're there to make a difference, not to make blunders. If only you had someone who could help you until your week-long training arrives. If only you had a sage coach who could guide you along with learned wisdom. Well, help is here.

You hold in your hands *The New Supervisor's Coach*. Written in a story format for ease of digestion and application, you will be guided through some of the most challenging situations a new supervisor can face. The exercises will help you immediately apply the story, concepts, and best-practices to your workplace.

The employee challenges are real. Compiled from the actual experiences of hundreds of participants in Dennis' supervisory training classes, you will learn to deal with eight very common employee challenges. Before you do, though, you will need to address two higher priorities.

Read on to discover the top three priorities of new supervisors as they start a new position.

Pat's Dilemma
Chapter 1 – The Coach's Plan

Pat, a new supervisor of three months, walked into her manager's office a little before 5:00 PM. "Keri, may I speak with you for a moment?" she asked with a disheartened tone.

"Sure, sit down," Keri said as she searched Pat's face. "You look beat; what's wrong?"

"You know I want to do a great job in my new position and make a real impact, but I have several employee issues that I don't have the least idea how to address."

"Go on," Keri said. "Tell me what's happening."

"In a nutshell, it's overwhelming when every person on your team has a unique challenge all at the same time."

"Everyone?" Keri responded.

"Well, it sure seems like it," answered Pat.

"You've got all the time you need. Tell me what's happening and I'll see how I can help."

Pat took a deep breath and began, almost as if she were reciting a list:

"First, I have an employee who is retiring in three years and has lost any motivation he had for the job. He gives just enough to barely meet expectations.

"Then there is Don who is quite a bit older than I am. He treats me like a kid fresh out of college.

"Jerry is a new-hire that performed so well before he completed probation, but now he's consistently late with lousy work. He's like a Dr. Jekyll and Mr. Hyde.

"Tawana needs constant reassurance that she is appreciated and has even said that I don't appreciate her.

"Lorraine is sarcastic and doesn't seem to respect anyone. Almost the entire staff refuses to work with her.

"As you know, Carlos works remotely in Sacramento. I don't know how to supervise him because I never see him.

"And last but not least, I have an employee with so many personal problems that her work performance is now affected by tardiness and excessive absenteeism."

Keri, looking genuinely shocked, said, "Wow, that is a lot to handle all at once, especially for a new supervisor."

"Oh yeah, and John accused me of favoritism last week when that couldn't be further from the truth!" Pat was clearly exasperated. "I'm sorry Keri. I feel like a whiner, but please help me with how to handle all of this. I've got some ideas, but I'm overwhelmed!"

"First, there is no need to apologize when I'm the one who should," Keri started. "I've been meaning to continue our one-on-one meetings since I returned from that Sacramento trip last month. I'm sorry that I didn't make it a higher priority...but it's not too late!"

She continued, "Second, I understand why you feel overwhelmed because I was in a similar situation as a new supervisor. It didn't hit all at once, but during my first couple of years I encountered just about all of these challenges. I learned a lot from the experience, so I can help. Think of me as your coach—someone who guides you along the way to success."

"A coach?" Pat seemed skeptical. "Now that's an image. I hope you don't mean like my high school cross-country coach who sent us on a seven-mile run while he 'encouraged' us from his pickup."

Keri laughed and said, "Well, if that's what it takes!" Then she thought for a moment and said. "No, I mean like *my* role model and favorite teacher, Coach Martinez. He would kneel down on one knee, give us that crooked smile, and, with empathy and support, guide us in the way things ought to be done."

"That sounds like some coach!"

"The man was amazing," Keri continued. "We got specific instruction and a lifted spirit all at once. Now, I'm no Coach Martinez, but I'm working on it; he's been my role model since junior high school."

Pat laughed gently and said, "So, do I call you Coach Keri?"

"Well, I do like the sound of that," Keri answered. She paused for a moment, pulled a pad of paper from her drawer and said, "Okay, here's the approach I'd like to take. We're going to go through Job 1, Job 2, and Job 3. In other words, to get you where you need to be, there are three jobs that must be done."

"Three jobs? I thought I needed to focus on being a good supervisor," Pat sounded dubious.

"By jobs I mean that in your job as a supervisor, you have three main areas or priorities to focus on," Keri responded. "Many supervisors focus on fixing employees without even thinking of two higher priorities."

Keri began scribbling. She wrote down "Job 1", "Job 2", and "Job 3" in large letters horizontally across the page and put big circles around each. In the first circle, she wrote "Work on the BOSS" and said,

"Work on the boss. Pat, that's you; *you're* Job 1." Pat opened her mouth to respond, but Keri was still talking. "Before you say that you're not the problem, let me say that you're not the problem. I'll explain later why you're Job 1."

She wrote "Work on the ENVIRONMENT" in the second circle and continued. "Job 2 is work on the environment. While people can be the problem, many performance issues are systemic. Some environments produce problem employees."

In the third circle she wrote, "Work on the EMPLOYEES" and said, "You're probably wondering what you got yourself into. You're probably thinking that you've got some challenging employees and that they're the real source of the problem. While you're partly right, I'd like you to trust me by letting us address the first two jobs and then work on the employees last."

"Okay," Pat responded hesitantly. "I trust your judgment. It's just that I have all these employee issues that seem to need immediate action."

"I understand. My approach will make a lot of sense after a session or two," Keri explained. "Besides, coaching and your development take time. When you see me making the investment, you'll feel better about your investment."

"Let's get going then!" Pat had definitely perked up.

"Well, I don't want to overwhelm you more than you are already, but I want to give you the urgency and attention that you need. I'm thinking that we meet for an hour twice a week at first. Then, after about four or five weeks, we can assess whether once a week is enough. What do you think?"

"I think that sounds very generous of you; thanks for working with me. I really appreciate your time."

"You're welcome, but it's my job. I promoted you. I can't let my new supervisor languish!" Keri exclaimed lightheartedly. "So, what time are you available tomorrow? I've got a half hour at 9:00 and an hour at 3:30."

Pat looked at her calendar. "Let's see; I've got something at 3:30, but I'll move it. This is really a priority for me."

"Great. I'll plan on seeing you here at 3:30," Keri said.

As Pat got up to leave, Keri chuckled a little and said, "Remember that hellish Tahoe project we worked on together?"

Pat laughed too and said, "How could I forget?"

"You know by now there's nothing that can get in our way. Don't worry. We're going to work through all of this together!"

"Thanks Keri; I'm looking forward to it," Pat said. "See you tomorrow."

Job 1 – Work on the Boss
Chapter 2 – Be a Person of Character

The next day, Pat rearranged her schedule to be sure she was early to her meeting at Keri's office. She walked briskly and had a spring in her step as she made her way there.

Noticing Pat's improved visage, Keri commented brightly, "Hey Pat! You must be feeling better."

"I sure do," Pat replied. "Just knowing that I'm not alone on this is huge. I slept much better last night…and we haven't even started!"

"That's the spirit! I guess the old 'Pat and Keri Show' is back," Keri said, laughing. "Let's get started."

"I'm ready." Pat's tone was excited but resolute.

"Okay," Keri began. "Let me start by explaining what I meant yesterday by Job 1—work on the boss. Before you start working on performance issues with the individuals on your team, your employees must respect you and believe in you. What do you think would happen if you started working on their performance before you worked on yours?"

Pat thought about the question. "To be honest, Keri, I didn't think I had any performance issues. I thought you promoted me because I was consistently rated outstanding on my performance reviews."

"That's true, and thanks for your honesty. In one sense, you're right about your performance, but some of that is irrelevant now. Consider your new position as supervisor. This is a whole new role for you. Are you on a learning curve? Are you able to handle the challenging performance issues on your team without some help?"

"Okay. I see your point."

"So, what do you think would happen if you started working on their performance before you worked on yours?" Keri asked.

Pat answered, "They would probably think, 'Who do you think you are correcting us?'"

"Yes" said Keri. "Now don't get me wrong. If there are blatant issues such as tardiness, absenteeism, and divisiveness, then those are issues that can't wait. Other issues that aren't so 'black and white' can wait while you 'sweep in front of your own house,' so to speak. Establishing yourself as a credible leader will position you to address their issues. While there are many factors in respect, none are more important than credibility. Are you seen by your team members as credible, believable?"

"Well, let me think about that." Pat paused for a moment. "I suppose they do, but I'm not really sure."

Keri asked another question. "Do they willingly follow you without coercion?"

"Some do, but now that you bring it up, it seems that several act like they have to—like they don't really want to."

Keri reassured Pat, "Every new manager has to deal with the credibility issue. It's the foundation of respect and trust, which are the keys to influencing others in positive ways. When individuals follow the leader because they have to—merely out of deference for the supervisor's position—it's a sign that the leader lacks credibility."

"That makes sense," Pat said.

"I hope it's clear I'm not saying that there's something wrong with you. I wouldn't have promoted you if I didn't think you were qualified and showed great potential. Not only do I believe that you will be an effective supervisor, but you have the potential of making significant impact at high levels in the organization. What I am saying is that the situation of being a new supervisor, especially one promoted among team members, is a situation in which credibility doesn't always come naturally."

"I haven't thought of that before," Pat said, "but it makes complete sense. Because I'm new in this position, some will not find me credible or trustworthy. It's almost like I'm a stranger who has to prove herself."

"Think of someone you trust besides a close family member. Why do you trust them?" Keri asked.

"Well, there could be several reasons, but I suppose it's because they do what they say they'll do."

"Exactly," answered Keri. "Now, are you ready to start talking about Job 1?"

"Sure am!" said Pat.

Keri pulled out a sheet of paper and began drawing, as she had done the day before. She wrote "Job 1" at the top of the page followed by "Work on the BOSS", then said:

"Whether you're creating respect 'from scratch' or building on some existing level of respect, there are three major actions you must take. When you answered the question of trust a moment ago, you were talking about the first one: be a person of character. We'll take a look at that and then two more: address promotion issues and create a positive culture."

Job 1 = Work on the BOSS		
☐ Action 1 Be a person of character	☐ Action 2 Address promotion issues	☐ Action 3 Create a positive culture

Pat looked at the list and nodded her head in agreement.

Keri said, "Let's take a look at the first major action you must take. You can be the most experienced supervisor or competent expert in the world, but if your character is not consistent with your words, your success will depend on political factors such as manipulation and favors. I know you don't want to go there because it's risky and doesn't fit your style." Pat nodded again and Keri continued:

"In a leadership position, who you are as a person matters much more than the techniques you use to influence others. Employees perform for leaders who consistently model the principles they have espoused."

"Try this exercise," Keri said as she handed Pat a piece of paper with a checklist on it. "Complete the following checklist by checking all of the principles you have communicated to your team."

Communicate What's Most Important

I have *communicated* the importance of the following principles:

☐ Honesty/integrity
☐ Fairness (consistency in applying standards)
☐ Learning from mistakes
☐ Continuous improvement
☐ Valuing people as individuals
☐ Energy; strong work ethic
☐ Persistence

When Pat only checked two of the boxes and looked at Keri sheepishly, Keri laughed and said, "Don't feel bad if you didn't check many boxes. Many supervisors don't talk about their values or principles—they would rather model them. If they had to make a choice between talking and walking, most leaders would choose walking. However, walking the talk involves walking *and* talking. Have you heard of a book called *The Leadership Challenge*? The authors discovered, through some of the most comprehensive research on leadership, that the walk is much more impressive when we talk about it first."

Pat's eyes lit up. "Aha! Now I know why you're always talking about those principles in staff meetings and planning sessions."

"Guilty as charged," Keri laughed and flipped the page over to reveal another checklist. "Okay. Here's the second part of the exercise: complete the following checklist by checking all of the principles you have modeled to your team."

Model What's Most Important

I have *consistently modeled* the following principles:

☐ Honesty/integrity
☐ Fairness (consistency in applying standards, policies, procedures)
☐ Learning from mistakes
☐ Continuous improvement
☐ Valuing people as individuals
☐ Energy; strong work ethic
☐ Persistence
☐ I have admitted visible mistakes and acknowledged recommitment to the principles above.

Pat smiled when she looked up from the page. All but two of the boxes were marked. "Well, that feels a lot better than the last checklist."

"When you talk about what is most important to you, your employees will watch you closely to see if you're for real. When they see you walking the talk, the positive impact to your team is greater than if you simply walked without talking first."

"Keri," Pat responded, "this makes a lot of sense. Although I believe I am a person of character, there is a huge opportunity for me to build my credibility more quickly and effectively."

"Then this is a good time for an action plan. As you know, when you find something of value and want to use it on the job, then create an action plan that you commit to follow through on and complete. To make a positive change, I've found this formula useful: ability + commitment + action = results."

Pat wrote the formula down on the piece of paper they were working from earlier.

Job 1 = Work on the BOSS		
☐ Action 1 Be a person of character	☐ Action 2 Address promotion issues	☐ Action 3 Create a positive culture
Ability + Commitment + Action = Results		

"Okay. Let's get to work on that action plan," Keri suggested.

Keri added a couple of column headings to the page, handed the piece of paper back to Pat, and said, "In the table below, write some actions and make a commitment to complete them within a certain timeframe."

Pat went to work on the grid. After a couple of minutes, she looked up from the page. "Keri, here's what I came up with. What do you think?"

Action	When
Make a list of what's most important to me and my team and post it in my cubicle	Today
Talk about what's most important in staff meetings, one-on-one meetings, and whenever it's appropriate/relevant	Tomorrow
Put a check mark next to any item on my list that I model	Ongoing

Keri looked the list over and said, "I can tell you've written an action plan before—great job! Is there anything that could keep you from completing these actions?"

"Nothing I can think of," said Pat.

"Great! We'll follow up on your action plan for Action 1 over the next few weeks to see how you're progressing. Next time we meet, we'll start on Action 2."

Chapter 3 – Address Promotion Issues

Keri began the next meeting leading a discussion of progress on Action1, but soon moved on to Action 2. "Pat, many new supervisors who are promoted from within a group face three challenges: friends, competitors, and strained relationships.

"In general, it is better to talk openly about a situation than to ignore it and hope everything will be fine. Open and honest communication will indicate that you are a supervisor who takes the initiative to make things better.

"In each situation, the following specific actions could save you a lot of trouble down the road. Please take a few moments to read the suggestions in the three situations and then let me know what you think."

Friend

Here are some steps to take when a former co-worker is a close friend. Before the promotion, meet with the friend and:

- Ask if he/she has any concerns about you going for the promotion.

- Explain that if you get the promotion, you will still be friends.

- Explain that being friends doesn't mean you'll treat him/her differently at work than the others on the team. For example, you won't be able to show any kind of favoritism.

After the promotion, meet with the friend and:

- Explain that you will have to be careful to keep some information confidential.

- Discuss the fact that you will need to give feedback about his/her performance. You will be honest and will welcome his/her feedback as well.

Competitor

Here are some steps to take when a former co-worker competed with you for the supervisory job. After your promotion, meet with the competitor and:

- Explain that you want a positive relationship and you want to discuss any concerns that may interfere.

- Recognize the person's strengths and experience and discuss how they will benefit the team.

Strained Relationship

Here are some steps to take when a former co-worker and you had negative conflict. After your promotion, meet with this person and:

- Tell him/her that you have put the past behind you and will work on developing a positive relationship.

- Have a rich discussion in which you both set mutual expectations. Discuss whether or not you are able to deliver the employee's expectations. If not, discuss why you are not able to and resolve the issues.

After reading the suggestions for the three situations, Pat was dejected. "I wish I had thought about these ahead of time. I've got all three of these on my team! As you know, Tawana and I have been friends for years. I wish we had sat down for a talk before the promotion, but at least we talked afterwards. More importantly, I wish I had talked to Don and John after I got the promotion. Who knows? Maybe some of our problems are related to competition or a strained relationship."

Keri replied, "I think that's very likely."

"Well, is it too late?" Pat asked.

"I think it is too late for these suggestions," Keri said apologetically. "Going forward, doing Job 1 and Job 2 will make up for missing these opportunities with Don and John. Remembering these for your next promotion will help you avoid future issues."

Chapter 4 – Create a Positive Culture

"Okay. We've only got 15 minutes left in this meeting," said Keri. "We better keep moving."

"Sounds good," said Pat. "I think I've just about filled my plate with Job 1 as it is!"

"I know, I know," Keri said empathetically. "It's a lot for the first meeting, but you'll have a good list of concrete actions to take when you leave here…"

"…and I'm not complaining!" Pat interrupted. "In fact, I'm really enjoying this. I'm really excited about the next item. How did you phrase that again?" She looked at the sheet in front of her. "That's right. Action 3 is 'Create a positive culture.'"

Keri went on. "The true culture of your team is one of the best indicators of your ability to manage and lead your team. What do you think I mean by culture?"

"Are you talking about the shared values and practices that characterize my team?" asked Pat.

"Yes!" exclaimed Keri. "That's a great definition. It may be too early to answer this question, but here's something to think about: what word or phrase would your employees use to describe the culture of your team?"

"Well, that's kind of a scary thought right now. The team seems so dysfunctional. I'm sure the words would not be very positive."

"Well, we're here to change all that," Keri said brightly. "Here's the next thing I'd like you to do: complete the following checklist by checking all of the boxes that are true of your team's culture."

Culture Checklist

Culture guides behavior and can either support or hamper a positive environment. My organization's culture:

- ☐ Is communicative (shares and listens)
- ☐ Cares about people as individuals
- ☐ Is consistent with my character
- ☐ Is consistent with my vision of where I want the team to be
- ☐ Consistently supports job performance (recognizes good performance and addresses poor performance)

When Pat was finished, Keri said, "Based on your comments earlier, it would be understandable if you didn't check any of the boxes. The important thing is that when you revisit this list in three months, six months, and a year, you will do much better. For now, envision what you want the team to be, not what you want the team to do. What you want the team to do will come later in Job 2. What you want the team to be needs to be written down, reflected on, and acted upon. It is a vision that you work toward every day, consistently doing something that will take you closer to the items on your checklist and a positive culture that motivates the team."

Pat's face went blank. "As much as I'm enjoying this, I'm beginning to feel overwhelmed. I'm not sure where to start."

"Do you mind if I take a first pass on your action plan?"

"That would be great."

Keri started to work on Pat's action plan and then stopped after a few seconds. "I can't believe I'm writing your action plan. That's the manager in me coming out. I'm supposed to be your coach who guides you through various challenges. There are times when the manager is supposed to take charge and make it happen. This isn't one of those times. I apologize; let's try this again. What goal or objective do you want for your team?"

"As we've been discussing, I'd like to create a positive culture."

Keri asked, "To change the culture of a team, what needs to happen?"

"Well, first, I need to define that positive culture. I like the checklist that I worked on earlier. That's better than anything I would create."

"Okay, that's the starting point. Using the same action plan format we used earlier, write the first action in the first column and a reasonable time to complete it in the second column."

Pat took a minute to complete the first row of the action plan and asked, "What's next?"

Keri answered with a question. "Well, after you've defined the positive culture, what else would help to change it?"

Pat asserted, "I need to take steps to model or reflect that culture."

"Yes, and how will you know you're modeling that culture?"

"Okay, I see what I need to do. You've given me enough guidance to finish it. Would you like me to do that now or take it as homework?"

"We've got the time now. Go ahead; I can check my voicemails while you complete your plan. Let me know if you have questions."

After a few minutes Pat proudly revealed her plan.

Action	When
Define the culture by creating a culture checklist in Excel and monitoring progress. The checklist will have two columns, one for the checkbox items from page 17 and the other for steps to achieve that item.	Today
When I take a step, I'll put a check mark to the right of the corresponding step.	Ongoing
After several check marks next to some of the steps, share the vision with the team & ask for their help. Note their responses & share progress in staff and 1-on-1 meetings.	When appropriate
Check a box when you feel you believe it's true of your team's culture.	When appropriate

Keri read the plan and said, "That's great! And the best part: it's yours, not mine. You're on a roll and I'd like to see you sustain the momentum, so I'm going to suggest that we do something a little different. Would you take a few minutes right now to create the Excel culture checklist?"

Pat asked, "You mean go to my cubicle now and work on it?"

"Yes, just come back here when you're done and we'll discuss the results."

Pat left for her cubicle and created the culture checklist. She printed copies for the two of them and returned to Keri's office.

Pat's Culture Checklist:

Culture Characteristic	Step(s) I will take and ✓ when I take a step	✓ True
Is communicative (shares and listens)	I will promote two-way communication in staff meetings by asking questions. I will check in with each individual on my team daily to see if I can help.	
Cares about people as individuals	I will make an effort to get to know each person better on my team.	
Is consistent with my character	At staff meetings and one-on-ones, I will check in for status: "How am I doing walking the talk?"	
Consistently supports job performance (recognizes good performance and addresses poor performance)	I will address performance issues in a timely manner with a coaching approach. When I see it, I will acknowledge good work with a specific "thank you."	
Is consistent with my vision of where I want the team to be	I will share my culture vision and check in with the team on examples of progress.	
I have asked for my team's assistance in creating this culture.	I will make this a staff meeting agenda item at least once a month.	

"Very impressive!" Keri exclaimed after reading through the checklist. "Your steps make sense and make it come alive. I don't want to put a damper on this, but I want to check in with you on a key to your success. How will you find the time to do all of this?"

Pat paused for a moment and answered, "I'll set aside time in the Calendar feature of Outlook. I learned a long time ago that if it isn't scheduled, it probably won't get done."

"This is solid all the way around. A solid plan and a solid handle on finding the time to do it. You might as well say goodbye to the dysfunctional team!"

"So this is what work on the boss means," Pat thought aloud. "It's not about fixing the boss as much as it is about creating a positive, open, and collaborative culture."

"You've got it," said Keri. "I'm looking forward to our next meeting. Now, go forth and conquer!" She laughed at herself when she realized she sounded a little cheesy.

Job 2 – Work on the Environment
Chapter 5 - Overview

A week later, it was time to move on to Job 2.

"Pat, before we start on Job 2, how is Job 1 going?" Keri asked as she pulled a notepad out of her drawer.

"Very well, I think," Pat said. "I'm progressing on both action plans and the culture checklist. Besides feeling good about making progress, just taking action gives me more confidence. I think the team can sense some positive changes, which builds my credibility."

"That's great," Keri responded, "I'm impressed with you for coming to me and applying the results of our discussions."

Pat smiled confidently as Keri continued, "Let's start on Job 2 and begin working on the environment."

As was her custom, Keri started writing on the notepad in front of her. She wrote "Job 2" followed by "Work on the ENVIRONMENT" across the top. She then added the items for Pat to work on.

Job 2 = Work on the ENVIRONMENT		
☐ Action 1 Set goals/clear expectations	☐ Action 2 Write a development plan for each employee	☐ Action 3 Make the necessary tools and resources available
☐ Action 4 Give meaningful feedback	☐ Actions 5 Address issues	☐ Action 6 Give written performance appraisals

"Now that you're focusing on you and ensuring a positive culture," Keri began, "we'll begin focusing on the environment. We need to do this before we get to Job 3, 'Work on the Employees,' which is where most managers want to start.

"Basically," Keri continued, "you must ensure that you've done everything you can to provide for employee success, which includes being a credible supervisor and setting up a performance environment. Too many supervisors come into a new group and start straightening out everyone else. This frustrates employees. All they see is a supervisor who is not self-aware and is not invested in their work performance.

"I've prepared another checklist for you to consider. This one will help you to focus on those areas needing your attention. Complete the following checklist by checking all of the boxes that you have adequately provided in the last year."

Pat was bewildered. "In the last year? I've only been a supervisor for three months!"

"I know," said Keri. "That's okay. This is a checklist you can revisit over time to check your progress. The reason I said one year is because in searching for success, some supervisors go two or more years back. That's too long. A supervisor may have adequately provided something two years ago, but it probably needs updating. Thinking of just the last year will help ensure that there is a focus on continuous reassessment and improvement. It may not need updating, but we won't know unless we look at recent actions taken in the last year."

"I see. That makes sense. Well, being new, I'm not sure I'll check any of them, but I'll consider the list."

Performance Environment Checklist

A performance environment has the following minimum elements:

- ☐ Goals / clear expectations
- ☐ Development plan
- ☐ Tools and resources
- ☐ Meaningful feedback
- ☐ Performance issues addressed promptly
- ☐ Written performance appraisals

When Pat had finished looking at the list, she said, "As I suspected, there isn't much checked."

"That's okay," said Keri. "Even if you checked them all, it's still a good idea to look at everything on the checklist. After all, a typical word in the English language has five definitions. There may be disconnects in the words we use."

"I've heard that before," said Pat. "Besides, I really want to get your perspective on performance management. I really haven't read any books or considered what it entails."

"That's why we're here!" said Keri. "There's a lot for a new supervisor to consider. Let's consider goals and expectations first."

Chapter 6 – Clear Expectations

"Performance planning is the usual starting point for an employee and supervisor to begin the performance management process," explained Keri. "They should meet, discuss, and agree on performance goals for the year. The bottom line of the planning process is that the supervisor and the employee should be able to answer four questions in the same way. What are the employee's major responsibilities for the year? How will the responsibilities be measured for success? Why is the employee doing what he/she is doing? How will the supervisor and employee communicate and work together to prevent problems and overcome barriers?

"Answers to the first two questions can be formalized as goals for more clarity. I suggest that you formalize your expectations as goals. Let's take a look at how to do that."

Pat had been taking notes, but began drawing pictures as she nodded for Keri to continue. Keri's "drawing thing" was rubbing off on Pat.

"Performance goals have two main elements. The first is a result. Basically, what is the outcome? The second main element is a measurement, some sort of indicator or metric to help both parties assess performance."

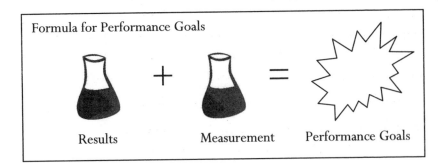

Formula for Performance Goals

Results + Measurement = Performance Goals

Keri looked over at Pat's notepad and smiled.

"Wow. I think I've created a monster!" she said.

They both laughed and Keri continued. "A result is a tangible outcome or output you want the employee to achieve. What are some examples of tangible results?"

Pat wrote down some ideas, then Keri added a second column and explained. "This should illustrate the difference between tangible results and activities."

Example (tangible result)	Non-Example (actions only)
• Closed cases	• Work on caseload
• Completed Issue Memo	• Research issue
• Healthier diet	• Eat more broccoli

"Okay," Keri said. "After you have a list of desired results, how will you know the result has been achieved?"

"A measurement," replied Pat, looking at her notes.

"That's right," said Keri. "A measurement states the criteria that will be used by the supervisor and the employee to validate achievement of an agreed-upon result. It also enables both parties to know if things are going well and will be finished as agreed upon. Keep in mind that there may be more than one measurement per result."

"That sounds good," said Pat. "What are some typical measurements?"

"Good question. Go ahead and write these down:

•Time   •Quantity   •Cost   •Quality

"What are some examples for each?" asked Keri.

Pat thought for a moment. "Well, time could include due dates or processing times. Quantity could be production numbers. Cost is easy; that's money. I guess quality is the absence or lack of errors."

"Perfect," said Keri. "Now let's use your list of results and add a measurement for each."

Result	Measurement
• Closed cases	• All priority cases closed by 12/15
• Completed Issue Memo	• Management sign-off by 10/30
• Healthier diet	• No fast food restaurants and no chips during the work week

"That's pretty easy," said Pat. "All I have to do is state the goal as a result or desired outcome, then state the measurement that represents the goal."

"Yes," said Keri. "Let's write another one for practice." She had Pat draw up a grid.

"Working alone, think of an example of work assigned to you or work that you assigned an employee. Using that example, write a clear performance goal that includes a result and at least one measurement."

Result	Measurement(s)

When Pat finished, Keri said, "When you've written the goal, it's not a bad idea to test the goal for clarity: if people met the measurement, would I be satisfied that they achieved the desired result? If yes, then you're done. If not, go back and make needed changes."

Keri continued, "Once your goals pass the clarity test, communicate them to everyone involved, and then meet with your employees on a regular basis to discuss progress. It's very motivating for everyone to feel a sense of accomplishment."

Chapter 7 – Development Plan

"Okay. Next step," said Keri. "Once performance goals are set, it is crucial that we continue down the checklist. It is harmful to the employee and the organization if managers set goals and then fail to provide all the means necessary to accomplish them."

"Absolutely," agreed Pat. "That happened in my last job. It was frustrating to have expectations but no plan or support to acquire the necessary additional skills or knowledge."

"Remember one of our previous meetings when we discussed my expectations and goals for you?" asked Keri. "Did you feel that way then?"

"I did at first because I felt some level of panic about how I was going to meet them. Then we started working on my development plan, and I remember feeling better about your expectations."

"You've expressed one of the key reasons why development plans are so important. Do you remember that form we looked at to address your concerns?"

"Yes," Pat responded almost proudly. "In fact, I brought the form with me."

"Perfect! Let's take a look at it to make another point in our current discussion."

Pat pulled the form out of a folder and put it on the table.

"Just as you and I have created a written plan for your development, your employees need the same thing. Development plans help managers and employees in planning development and improvements, listing actions required to meet those developments and improvements, committing to an expected date of completion, and a column for reporting status."

"Since we created this, I've referred back to it often," remarked Pat.

"That's great!" said Keri. "It's a great tool for checking progress, especially for long-term goals that require your employees to have an expanded knowledge base or an improved skill set. It's also an excellent tool for career development."

Development Plan

EMPLOYEE NAME: Pat Edwards   REVIEW PERIOD: 4/10 to 10/10

Revision # 1

Improvements/ Developments	Actions	Due Date	Measurement	Status
Build credibility with your team members.	Make a list of what's most important to me and my team, and post it in my cubicle. Talk about what's most important in staff meetings, one-on-one meetings, and whenever it's appropriate.	5/20	List posted in cubicle. Add to staff meeting agenda for six months.	Done Ongoing
Create a performance environment for your team.	Clear expectations/goals set for team and team members.	6/15	Goals listed in June status report.	In progress
Increase basic supervisory knowledge.	Read "The One Minute Manager" and report key learnings.	7/1	Send report to Keri for discussion.	Book read Report in progress

"Like goals," Keri continued, "development plans need to be reviewed with employees regularly. Hold a formal meeting with each employee at least once a month to discuss progress toward goals and items on the development plan. Progress breeds success."

Chapter 8 – Tools and Resources

"Now," said Keri, "a plan is one thing, but what would it be like for me to give you a goal or set an expectation without the means to accomplish it?"

"Frustrating," Pat answered. "It wouldn't be fair. I'd be set up for failure."

"That's how your employees would feel too. Did you know that is one of the main reasons employees leave their jobs?"

"I've heard that. It's why I left my last job," Pat said grimly.

Keri nodded in support. "Well, their loss is our gain! That's why this part of performance management is so vital. Managers are responsible for providing necessary tools and resources. Employees are responsible for providing input to the manager with regard to their needs. Being closer to the work provides employees with a clearer picture of the tools and resources needed to do the job.

"If employees understand your expectations, they often can tell you what tools and resources they need to meet expectations. It's a good idea to encourage employees to meet with you and discuss their needs on a regular basis no matter how busy it may be."

Pat made a note on her calendar. "That's a great idea; I'll ask them what they need as a group at the next meeting and encourage them to meet with me individually too."

"Good," said Keri as she handed Pat a piece of paper, "and it would help to use this form because it will spark their thoughts, encourage input, and provide a record for all to see. Take a moment to read it; let me know if you have questions."

"Thanks," Pat said as she took the form. "Can you send me a soft-copy?"

"Of course!"

Tools and Resources We Need in the Next Year	
Tool/resource	Details/information
Software	
Hardware	
Online documentation/manuals	
Equipment	
Job aids	
Supplies	
On-the-job training / cross training	

After looking the form over, Pat asked, "What if they suggest something that costs too much or isn't in the budget for this year?"

"That's a good question," Keri said. "Create a plan for providing what's lacking and if there isn't enough money, explain why it will have to wait. Make sure to have a follow-up meeting to review the plan and provide explanations. Review the plan periodically to show progress and keep it current. This is one more way to build your credibility."

Chapter 9 – Meaningful Feedback

Keri pulled out the notepad with the Job 2 drawing. After checking off Actions 1-3, Keri said, "I don't know about you, but time is flying; we're already on Action 4!"

Job 2 = Work on the ENVIRONMENT

☑ Action 1 Set goals/clear expectations	☑ Action 2 Write a development plan for each employee	☑ Action 3 Make the necessary tools and resources available
☐ Action 4 Give meaningful feedback	☐ Actions 5 Address issues	☐ Action 6 Give written performance appraisals

Pat nodded enthusiastically as Keri continued, "Giving feedback is serious business. Can you imagine employees trying to meet your expectations without feedback?"

"Yes," Pat said as she shook her head. "I've been there as an employee. It'd be a mess. They wouldn't know where to go or what to do."

"Let me tell you a story. A senior couple retired to Florida. One morning as Mabel was getting out of bed, she stopped before her feet were even on the floor and slowly reached around to shake her sleeping husband. In a drowsy voice he asked, 'What do you want?' She responded, 'Elmer, am I dead?' He responded in a confused tone, 'Of course not. Why?' to which Mabel replied, 'I must be. Nothing hurts this morning!'"

Pat gave Keri a courtesy laugh but looked confused.

"Well, I thought it was funny when I heard it," Keri said, "but it proves a point. It tells us that any feedback is good feedback."

"I get it now," Pat chuckled.

"Manager-based feedback provides information to the employee directly. In order to provide meaningful feedback, you should collect information pertaining to the employee's performance. Typical methods include:

- 1:1 meetings with the employee
- Direct observation
- Monitoring indicators, surveys, progress reports
- Feedback from others about the employee's performance

"Once you have collected performance data, provide feedback to the employee. Feedback can be positive if you want to reinforce good performance or constructive when you need to correct performance that is below expectations."

Pat shook her head as Keri finished. "My former boss was clueless to this information you're sharing. He rarely—if ever—gave positive feedback and his constructive feedback wasn't very constructive."

"You're not alone. Most employees have had a manager or supervisor who struggles with giving feedback at all, much less positive feedback. I'll send you an email with the next two items, but take a second to read over these guidelines for providing positive and constructive feedback. Then let me know if you have questions."

Positive Feedback

Be specific	Reference the specific performance you want to continue. General/vague feedback gives the perception that it's not sincere (e.g., "You're doing a good job").
Be positive	Encouragement should be free from correction. Criticism taints encouragement. People tend to remember the negative.
Keep it pure	Comment only about the good aspects of performance. Don't start out by saying something good and then move toward correction.
Spontaneous	When possible, give immediately after performance. Waiting too long after the event dilutes the message and weakens its impact.

Constructive Feedback

Undesired performance	Clearly explain the current performance you are trying to change. Be sure to give the employee an opportunity to comment on or disagree with your assessment.
Desired performance	Clearly explain what performance you want to see in the future. It's effective to contrast the undesired performance with the desired.
Timing	If possible, try to offer advice just before the employee has an opportunity to use it. This way, it's not perceived as criticism and it stays fresh when needed. Note: this may not always be appropriate (e.g., safety emergency).
One issue	Don't bring up multiple issues. Raising others may decrease the focus and give the impression of "piling on."
Check understanding	By asking the employee to respond to the advice, you will see if the employee understands and can commit.

When Pat finished reading the feedback guidelines she said, "I'm not sure I agree with the guideline about keeping it pure. It seems to me that there will be times when you will need to give positive *and* constructive feedback in the same conversation. For example, when you gave me a performance appraisal last year, I heard both types of feedback."

"Good point," said Keri. "There are some situations where the 'keep it pure' guideline won't be used, but when you're recognizing someone's good performance, it needs to be positive. The difference in my mind is recognition vs. evaluation. If you're evaluating someone's performance, whether it's a formal written appraisal, a PowerPoint presentation, or a customer service encounter, the situation requires two perspectives. If you're recognizing someone's good performance, the situation requires one perspective."

"Now that you put it that way, Keri, I see the difference. If I mixed recognition for a good job with constructive feedback, it would be like giving my husband a cordless drill for his birthday and then telling him that his work better improve with such a fine tool!"

They both had a good laugh and then Keri said, "It's amazing how many of these business guidelines apply in our personal lives too. I've found it helpful that there's a double benefit to what we do. That should help keep us motivated going forward. I'll see you next time, Pat. Keep up the good work."

Chapter 10 – Issues Addressed Promptly

"Okay. So what's next?" asked Pat.

"Well, since we just finished talking about feedback, let me ask you a question," said Keri. "What would happen if a performance issue—let's say tardiness—wasn't addressed with the employee?"

"It could create resentment and hurt morale. If others show up on time, but one individual flaunts the rules, resentment grows. That hurts morale and then others might start slipping in performance while using the one individual's behavior and lack of accountability as an excuse. It becomes a vicious cycle."

"Exactly," Keri responded encouragingly. "You hit that right on the head. Resentment will break down morale and destroy team unity. On top of that, ignoring performance issues hurts your credibility as the supervisor too."

"Well, we're not on Job 3 yet. Is that where we should talk about performance issues?" Pat asked.

"Yes and no. Until a supervisor has established credibility and a solid working rapport with the team, I suggest a two-stage approach for performance issues. During Job 1, it's a good idea to address blatant issues such as tardiness, attendance, divisiveness, lack of respect, and other serious problems of performance. Later, in Job 3—or maybe late in Job 2—you can begin to address the less serious performance issues."

Pat was nodding. "That makes sense. I can't ignore the really obvious, divisive stuff because it hurts my credibility."

"Can you think of any examples where you might put this into practice?" asked Keri.

"I think so," Pat said as she thought for a moment. "Well, it was a priority for me to address Meredith's attendance issue and Lorraine's disrespect issue. I thought that waiting to address those issues would make me look like a pushover. With Don's lack of respect, it wasn't totally blatant, so I thought it would make sense to gain credibility with him— Job 1, right?—and to work on Job 2 while taking a more patient approach. As I mentioned, he seems to be coming around and has started showing more respect for me without my ever having to talk to him. The only thing I take exception to would be some obvious sign of disrespect, like when others see him rolling his eyes. That has to be addressed right away."

"You've got it down," Keri said. "You've already figured out that there's a difference between earning respect over time and needing to address blatant disrespect immediately. Basically, for now, you need to address blatant or serious issues. By the time you get to Job 3, some issues will be resolved by proving your character and creating a positive environment that empowers team members—just doing Jobs 1 and 2 goes a long way!"

Chapter 11 – Written Performance Appraisals

Keri began, "Let's see where we are in our Job 2 actions." While checking off two more actions Keri noted, "We've completed the first five actions and we're ready for our last one!"

Job 2 = Work on the ENVIRONMENT		
☑ Action 1 Set goals/clear expectations	☑ Action 2 Write a development plan for each employee	☑ Action 3 Make the necessary tools and resources available
☑ Action 4 Give meaningful feedback	☑ Actions 5 Address issues	☐ Action 6 Give written performance appraisals

Keri switched gears and asked Pat a question. "Pat, did you go to your Senior Prom?"

Pat laughed and said, "Yes, but that's on odd question considering our topic!"

Keri smiled. "Maybe; but bear with me. Did you get dressed up in typical Senior Prom clothes?"

"Yes. Typical 80s fare. Ruffled dress, big shoulders, bigger hair. Now you've sparked my interest. Where is this going?"

"Just one more question. Why do people dress up at the Prom?"

"People dress up because it makes it a special occasion, only happens once a year, and will be remembered for years to come."

Keri nodded. "It's the same thing with performance appraisals. As you know, the performance appraisal is the formal written record of the employee's contribution for the past year. It should accurately and fairly summarize the employee's previous year's performance and outline areas for development over the coming year. That"—Keri smiled as she finished her analogy—"is what makes it a special occasion that will be remembered."

"Okay, okay. I get it," Pat laughed. "Of course, I didn't much enjoy my Prom...but that's not the point."

"You're right," Keri said. "The point is that the performance appraisal is the culmination of year-round performance management and development. Unlike a Prom, it shouldn't be the only occasion during the year in which the employee receives performance feedback. The content and message of the annual performance appraisal should never be a surprise."

"Since there is a strong correlation between the supervisor's feelings about written appraisals and the quality of what's written, let's do an exercise that should help form positive attitudes and beliefs. Take a moment to make a list of the benefits of a supervisor delivering quality written performance appraisals to her employees."

The Value of Appraisals

_____

_____

_____

_____

Pat took a couple of minutes and wrote a number of benefits on the page. When she finished, she passed the list to Keri.

Keri looked over the list and said, "You came up with a great list of benefits. Besides 'employee's contribution for the year is acknowledged' and 'employee understands areas to work on in the coming year,' I see you went back to our Prom analogy with 'feedback is understood in memorable ways.' That benefit reflects the formal nature of a written performance appraisal. When management takes so much time and puts so much effort into the appraisal, it's more likely to be understood and appreciated. You'll be writing your first review in a few months. I hope this helps you to produce a quality product that impresses your employees."

"I've heard some negative things about the process," admitted Pat, "but you've helped me to see the other side of the story."

"I'm glad," said Keri. "Now let's get into the nuts and bolts of writing and delivering a performance appraisal. Let's look at writing the performance appraisal first."

How to Write a Performance Appraisal

1. Guide employees to provide their own input:
   - o Provide a form for gathering employee feedback
   - o With the employee, review the writing guidelines in step 3 below

2. Gather performance information:
   - o 1:1 meetings with the employee
   - o Direct observation
   - o Monitoring indicators, surveys, progress reports
   - o Employee input (from step 1)

3. Write the appraisal:
   - o Integrate employee input and other sources of performance information
   - o Use a performance appraisal form (check with Human Resources or use the one in Appendix C)
   - o Adhere to the following writing guidelines:
     - o Include meaningful, job-specific examples
     - o Be concise – eliminate wordy expressions
     - o Edit feedback to maintain confidentiality
     - o Use specific examples of observable skills, behaviors, and knowledge
     - o Do not reference personal traits or job-protected leaves of absence
     - o Explain or avoid using abbreviations and acronyms

After going through the list, Keri asked "Do you have questions about any of these items?"

"I do, actually. What is meant by 'do not reference personal traits'?"

"Good question," answered Keri. "That means do not bring up anything that isn't work related behavior. For example, don't bring up 'good dresser' or 'pleasant smile' unless it relates directly to the job. Those aren't related to performance and can be awkward, not to mention unprofessional."

"That makes sense," said Pat.

"Okay. The second major section in the process is how to deliver a performance appraisal. Let's look at some guidelines."

How to Deliver a Performance Appraisal

1. Provide a copy to the employee several hours before oral delivery so the employee can reflect on it and ask quality questions.

2. Set the context for a meaningful delivery by reviewing the purpose of a performance appraisal as a tool. It is used to:

   o Communicate a performance message to the employee that is clear, honest, and direct

   o Acknowledge impact of an individual's accomplishments

   o Encourage continuous improvement

   o Provide accurate performance data

3. Adhere to the following guidelines:

   o Deliver the message in a location that preserves confidentiality

   o The message and tone should be consistent with the performance appraisal document

   o Ensure the message is based on a factual representation of the written review

"Do you have any questions about these?" Keri asked.

Pat asked, "What do you mean by 'the message and tone should be consistent with the document'?"

Keri answered, "That means you shouldn't have a tone in your voice that is inconsistent with your message. For example, don't have an upbeat/glowing tone if the message is not positive. Conversely, don't sound somber if the message is positive. The idea is to avoid a mixed message, which could confuse and even anger the employee."

"Got it," said Pat.

"There's a lot to the performance appraisal process," Keri said in a comforting tone. "Don't hesitate to ask questions of me or Maria, our HR representative. No one expects you to go through this process the first time alone. It's a lot of work, so don't forget your notes on page 39."

Job 3 – Work on the Employees
Chapter 12 – Supervisor as Coach

Over the ensuing weeks, Keri and Pat continued to meet to check progress on Pat's action plan, answer questions, and deal with issues that came up. Before long, they were ready to move on to Job 3.

"Pat, before we get started on Job 3, I want to check in with you on Job 2. How's it going?" Keri asked.

Pat smiled brightly and said, "Very well. I'm progressing on all the action plans and I see some positive changes in team members, and we haven't even started on the specific performance issues."

Keri inquired further. "Really, like who?"

"Take Don for example, the one who's quite a bit older and doesn't respect me. He's making more eye contact with me during staff and one-on-one meetings. He actually smiled at me when I made a suggestion the other day. And then there's Tawana, the one who doesn't feel appreciated by me. She isn't as whiny and isn't pointing out all the things she does for the team as much as she used to."

"That's great," said Keri. I'm very pleased that it's going so well. Thank you for coming to me and working hard to apply the results of our discussions. You are truly succeeding. Why do you think it's going so well?"

"Well," Pat said thoughtfully, "It seems that by working on the boss and the environment, some performance issues have solved themselves. I feel like people respect me more and see me as credible. Combined with a supportive environment, the staff seems more motivated to work better."

"That is music to my ears!" Keri said excitedly. "You've discovered a huge secret: most employee performance issues are a reaction to management. Most employees meet expectations when managers do their job and provide leadership. Job 3 is for those times when Job 1 and Job 2 aren't quite enough."

"That reminds me: as we embark on Job 3, don't forget to continue to work on Job 1 (the boss) and Job 2 (the environment). A good way to do this is to revisit your action plans at least once a year. In fact, that's an action plan in itself."

"Good point!" said Pat as she wrote down two action items on her list.

Action	When
Enter 12/28 in Outlook as a recurring appointment to review all action plans at least once a year.	Today, when I get back to my desk
Write action items to be carried out by the end of January (as a result of action plan review).	12/28

When she finished, Keri said, "Before we get into your first performance issue, I need to give you some background on my coaching approach. Most of the issues sound like coaching will be the best approach, so here's a good working definition:

"Coaching is an approach to management in which supervisors help employees to achieve their goals. Coaching draws out the best in a person and provides guidance and support. It is a more collaborative relationship, which is largely due to the shifting trend in management to empower and influence employees instead of directing their activities. Here's the bottom line: job performance is better when employees are guided and empowered rather than told what to do."

Pat was impressed. "It sounds like coaching is the magic potion to cure all performance issues."

"Well," said Keri, "it is a proven approach, but there are times when coaching doesn't work or isn't appropriate. Some issues may just require feedback; coaching could be overkill. Also, not everyone responds to coaching, but that's a rare exception. Some employees will only respond to the latter stages of corrective discipline. Even more rarely, termination is the only answer. As a rule, coaching works because you're working with the employee."

"I definitely prefer a collaborative approach," Pat said. "It sounds like most of the issues we're going to tackle are candidates for coaching."

"Great. Let's get started." Keri began writing on the page in front of her. She wrote "Job 3" and "Work on the EMPLOYEES" on the page, then filled in some boxes she drew.

<u>Job 3 = Work on the EMPLOYEES</u>		
☐ Action Coaching in the form of:	● OJT (on-the-job training)	● Encouragement
● Motivation	● Alignment	● Realignment

"Nearly all performance issues fall into one of these five opportunities:

OJT (On-the-job training)

- Provide OJT when someone doesn't have a job skill.

Encouragement

- Provide encouragement when someone has a job skill, but needs reassurance.

Motivation

- Provide motivation when someone is meeting expectations, but could do better based on his/her education, experience, and ability.

Alignment

- Provide alignment when someone doesn't meet expectations from time to time.

Realignment

- Provide realignment when someone consistently isn't meeting expectations.

"The first thing I'd like you to do is categorize your eight performance issues in one of the five coaching opportunities," Keri instructed as she handed Pat a piece of paper with a chart on it.

Pat paused briefly. "Why is it important to categorize them?"

"The coaching model I'll share with you is situational," explained Keri. "The way we coach OJT is different than coaching Encouragement and the way we coach Encouragement is different than coaching Motivation and so forth. By categorizing the different opportunities, we'll be able to take different approaches depending on the situation."

"I see. That makes sense. Thanks for explaining the thought behind it. So, what was it you wanted me to do?"

"Take a few minutes and match your employees' eight performance issues with the five opportunities of coaching in the following table."

Pat began working on the matching exercise. (Note to readers: see if you agree with Pat's results on the next page.)

Coaching Opportunity	Performance Issue
OJT: Provide OJT when someone doesn't have a job skill.	
Encouragement: Provide encouragement when someone has a job skill, but needs reassurance.	Tawana doesn't feel appreciated. Carlos is a remotely located employee.
Motivation: Provide motivation when someone is meeting expectations, but could do better based on education, experience, and ability.	Jack is doing the minimum; it may be related to his retirement in three years.
Alignment: Provide alignment when someone doesn't meet expectations from time to time.	Don doesn't respect younger supervisor. Jerry is Dr. Jekyll before probation and Mr. Hyde after probation.
Realignment: Provide realignment when someone consistently isn't meeting expectations.	Lorraine lacks respect for everyone. Meredith has many personal and family problems...affecting reliability.

After Pat filled in the chart, she asked Keri: "What do you think of my matching job? Keep in mind that I left one out: John perceives favoritism by supervisor. I thought it might be better to simply provide feedback in that situation."

Keri said, "I agree with you overall and I might agree with you completely if I understand your rationale. So, please provide your reasoning for each opportunity."

"Okay, here goes."

Coaching Opportunity	Performance Issue
Encouragement: Provide encouragement when someone has a job skill, but needs reassurance.	Tawana doesn't feel appreciated. Carlos is a remotely located employee.

"These two aren't really performance issues. They could be if not addressed proactively. When someone doesn't feel appreciated, they need more encouragement or confirmation. If ignored over time, Tawana may lose her motivation to work hard. Carlos is a very good performer, but employees who work in remote locations can begin to feel left out. If ignored over time, Carlos' performance may suffer because he doesn't feel supported."

Coaching Opportunity	Performance Issue
Motivation: Provide motivation when someone is meeting expectations, but could do better based on education, experience, and ability.	Jack is doing the minimum; it may be related to his retirement in three years.

"It seems like Jack is coasting. I think it's because he's three years from retirement, but maybe there's something else going on. Regardless, I put it here because he could be doing more. I didn't put him under Alignment because he's meeting expectations. Still, I need him to do more, especially considering the fact that he used to do more and I need him to set a good example because some team members look up to him."

Coaching Opportunity	Performance Issue
Alignment: Provide alignment when someone doesn't meet expectations from time to time.	Don is older...doesn't respect younger supervisor. Jerry is Dr. Jekyll before probation and Mr. Hyde after probation.

"Don is getting better as I mentioned earlier, but he still shows signs of disrespect toward me. I think it's because I'm younger, but maybe it's something else. Regardless, I put it here because it's wrong to disrespect anyone, and if ignored, it could spread to other team members. I understand the concept of earned authority, but if someone's attitude keeps a reasonable leader from earning authority, then it needs to be addressed. His productivity is fine, but I feel that his behavior needs to be aligned.

"Jerry isn't performing to expectations. I initially wanted to put him under Realignment because I have a feeling that's where we're going to end up, but I must try to align first."

Coaching Opportunity	Performance Issue
Realignment: Provide realignment when someone consistently isn't meeting expectations.	Lorraine lacks respect for everyone. Meredith has many personal and family problems...affecting reliability.

"Simply put, Lorraine is a difficult person. There's not a day that goes by in which she doesn't make a rude remark or try to put someone down. The team has nicknamed her 'Lorraine the Pain.' Her level of productivity is fine, but if her behavior is ignored, more and more team members will refrain from working with her. Everyone except John and Meredith has come to me, threatening to not work with her. I haven't used your coaching model, but I've talked to her about her lack of respect. I put her under Realignment because Alignment (at least my version of it) hasn't worked.

"Meredith has attendance issues due to her many personal/family problems. Again, I haven't used your coaching model, but I have talked to her about tardiness and excessive absence. I feel sorry for her, but I can't ignore her behavior. I put her under Realignment because Alignment (at least my version of it) hasn't worked.

"So...what do you think? Hit me with your best shot!" Pat laughed.

"Actually, that was excellent." Keri was genuinely impressed. "I wasn't sure about Carlos being under Encouragement, but that makes a lot of sense. This is a really good start. Now what about John who perceives favoritism on your part? Why do you think it might be better to simply provide feedback in that situation?"

"Well, I felt I needed to address it right away, so I did. I wasn't aware at that time about taking a coaching approach, so I simply talked to him about it. It turned out to be a misunderstanding. In fact, the talk seemed to take care of it."

"Congratulations! It's so great that you didn't ignore an uncomfortable situation. That's one of the reasons I thought you'd be great for this job. So, we can put that one 'on the back burner' for now. I'd like to revisit it after we've talked about coaching for the other situations. There may be an opportunity to talk about a best practice for giving feedback."

"Sounds good," answered Pat.

"There's one last thing before I share the coaching model with you and get to some specifics. Do you find it odd that nothing went under OJT?"

"Not really, because we don't have anyone new on the team that doesn't understand how to do their job. Jerry is the newest person on the team—almost 14 months. Don has pretty much completed all of the OJT with Jerry, and he proved his ability during probation. I'm not saying that at some point someone won't need OJT, but there aren't any new software upgrades or applications on the horizon. Should I be concerned that there's nothing under OJT?"

"Not at all! That was just the answer I was looking for. Okay, let's get into the model."

Chapter 13 – Situational Coaching Model

Keri handed Pat a sheet of paper that read "Situational Coaching Model" across the top.

Situational Coaching Model

	Steps	Opportunities

Before Coaching	1. Evaluate the situation
	  • Observe behavior and/or result
	  • Match the situation with one of the five opportunities (see page 47)
	  • Take notes on how you will approach the situation using the remaining steps as a guideline	

Coaching	2. Describe the situation
	  • Introduce the opportunity
	  • Discuss the impact
	  • Gain agreement that there is a situation that needs to be addressed
	
	3. Plan a change
	  • Collaborate on a solution
	  • Ensure understanding
	  • Gain commitment
	
	4. Revisit the plan
	  • Set a date
	  • Be supportive
		OJT
		Encouragement
		Motivation
		Alignment
		Realignment

Keri said, "The four-step model of effective coaching applies to all five of the opportunities we've listed. There are specific steps we'll look at that vary depending on the opportunity, but the four general steps apply to the five opportunities at a high level.

"For example, Step 3—plan a change—applies to all five opportunities. You will collaborate on a solution, ensure understanding, and gain commitment to a plan no matter what the opportunity. Then there are specific ways to carry out Step 3 depending on the opportunity. You'll notice how they differ as we work through each of the five coaching opportunities."

"Okay," said Pat. "Before we get to the specific situations and steps, it would help me to understand the four general steps a little better. Can you give me an overview?"

"Of course!" answered Keri. "Thanks for asking. Here's how they work:

- Step 1 is done on your own before you meet with the employee. It's important to not assume anything about a situation. This step is all about ensuring that you understand the situation as best you can before you start coaching at Step 2.

- Step 2 begins the coaching session. This step is all about coming to a mutual understanding of the situation. You did your homework in Step 1, but there may be something you don't know or haven't considered from the employee's perspective. You have completed Step 2 when you both agree on the nature of the problem or opportunity.

- Step 3 is all about coming to a mutual agreement about what to do. You have completed Step 3 when you both agree on next steps to address the problem or opportunity.

- Step 4 is all about follow-through. You have completed Step 4 when you both agree on when to meet for a progress report."

"I like its simplicity and how it flows," remarked Pat. "Thanks for taking the time to explain that to me. It's helpful to get a big-picture view of the model."

"You're right that it is simple in concept. Just know that you will be challenged by the complexity of people and their responses. What I really like about the model are these benefits:

- Helps the talkative supervisor to stay on task and not get off on tangents.

- Helps the new supervisor with assurance that they're coaching correctly.

- Helps the supervisor who avoids conflict to be assertive.

- Helps the impatient or brash supervisor to take a collaborative approach, listen, and help the employee feel supported."

"I can't wait to get started and feel the assurance that I'm coaching correctly," said Pat.

"Where do you want to start?" asked Keri.

"Well, I think I'd *like* to start with my two Realignment opportunities, but I think it's better to learn this model by beginning with the less challenging situations."

"The least challenging situations are OJT and Encouragement. Since you don't have someone who needs OJT, let's help the employees who need encouragement. Here are the specific steps for Encouragement."

(Note to readers: you can find the steps for coaching OJT in Appendix A on page 85).

Coaching Opportunity: Encouragement

Provide encouragement when someone has a job skill, but needs reassurance.

	Model Steps	Encouragement Steps
Before Coaching	1. Evaluate the situation	a. Observe behavior and/or result
		b. Match the situation with one of the five opportunities (see page 47)
		c. Take notes on how you will approach the situation using the remaining steps as a guideline
Coaching	2. Describe the situation	a. Describe what you've observed/heard
		b. Encourage the employee to respond
		• If appropriate, share a time when you needed encouragement
	3. Plan a change	a. Share some encouraging words
		b. Help employee discover his/her own confidence by asking how he/she has dealt with a tough situation in the past
		• Encourage employee to share from his/her past experience
		c. Demonstrate your confidence in the employee's ability by keeping him/her on the task/project
		d. Offer support/resources to help
	4. Revisit the plan	a. Set a date
		b. Be supportive

"Let's start with Tawana's situation. What's going on there?" asked Keri.

"She's meeting performance expectations, which is great, but I've got a not insignificant list of her complaints. She whines about giving so much to the team, but the team doesn't reciprocate. She points out all the things she does for the team, but the team doesn't appreciate her. She gossips about other team members. She has told me several times that I don't appreciate her enough."

"I'll play the devil's advocate," said Keri. "She's getting the work done, so why does it matter about the other things?"

"If her behavior is ignored over time," Pat said, "she may lose her motivation to work hard. Also, her gossiping could affect the morale of the team."

"Exactly," Keri said encouragingly. "Here's what I'd like you to do: I'd like you to complete a Coaching Worksheet for Tawana."

"Okay. What's a Coaching Worksheet?"

"It's a template that guides you to prepare for the employee coaching session," Keri explained. "As you can see, it includes the four main steps of the Coaching Model. Using the Encouragement Steps, you're going to write down what you will say in a coaching session with Tawana."

"Okay. Let's see if I've got this." Pat pointed to the different sections of the Encouragement Model as she spoke. "On the Coaching Worksheet on the next page, I write my analysis of the situation in Step 1 and then write what I will say for Steps 2, 3, and 4. I'll know what to write by referring to the Encouragement Steps instructions on the right side of the model."

"Perfect!" said Keri. "I'll review it when you're done."

Coaching Worksheet – How would you coach Tawana?

1. Evaluate the situation

2. Describe the situation

3. Plan a change

4. Revisit the plan

Coaching Worksheet Example – Possible Results for Tawana

1. Evaluate the situation
   - She complains about giving so much to the team especially when the team doesn't reciprocate.
   - She gossips about other team members.
   - She has told me several times that I don't appreciate her enough.

2. Describe the situation
   - "Tawana, I want to talk to you about how we can improve our working relationship."
   - "I've given some thought about your statement that I don't appreciate you enough. I want to understand why you feel this way." (Pause; allow Tawana to respond.)
   - "Also, you think that team members don't appreciate you enough. Tell me more about why you feel this way."

3. Plan a change
   - "I may not show it sufficiently, but I appreciate you for the following reasons…"
   - "Besides our team, tell me about a time you've felt unappreciated in the past."
   - "How did you deal with it?"
   - "We all have a responsibility to show our appreciation to others. However, that won't always happen. Is there something you can do to help improve the situation?"
   - "That's a good idea. Is there anything I can do to assist you?"

4. Revisit the plan
   - "Let's get back together so I can hear from you how things are going. When is a good time for you in the next two weeks?"

After Pat spent a few minutes filling out the worksheet, she and Keri went over the results together.

"I like your coaching approach for Tawana," said Keri. "I think she'll feel supported and appreciated by you. If the gossiping continues, you may have to address that separately as Alignment, but hopefully that won't be necessary. How do you feel about this?"

Pat smiled and said, "I really like this approach. It helps to sit down and do a thorough analysis of the situation, not to mention prep for what could be an uncomfortable meeting."

"I'm glad that helped. Let's move on to Carlos. He's another employee who needs encouragement. Remind me about his situation."

Pat said, "Carlos is remotely located in Sacramento. It's a long story about why he's not here in San Diego, but the important thing is that supervising remotely located employees has a special set of challenges. He's a very good performer, but I think he's beginning to feel left out. If ignored over time, Carlos' performance may suffer because he doesn't feel supported."

"Okay Pat. You know what to do next."

"Fill out a Coaching Worksheet for Carlos?" Pat asked.

"Absolutely. Let me know when you're done."

Coaching Worksheet — How would you coach Carlos?

1. Evaluate the situation

2. Describe the situation

3. Plan a change

4. Revisit the plan

Coaching Worksheet Example – Possible Coaching Results for Carlos

1. Evaluate the situation
   - He works out of his home in Sacramento by himself.
   - He comes down to San Diego once a month to touch base and attend one staff meeting out of four per month.
   - I don't think he experiences face-to-face synergy of the team.
   - How will Carlos observe me? I like to manage by walking around. How will Carlos see my style?
   - Teleconference is not a very good way to communicate with staff during meetings.

2. Describe the situation
   - "Carlos, I want to talk about how we can improve our working relationship."
   - "It seems that distance can make people feel disconnected. Technology helps, but we miss out so much when there's very little face-to-face communication. I'm concerned that you may feel disconnected from the team." (Pause; allow Carlos to respond.)

3. Plan a change
   - "You are a valuable part of this team. I don't want you to feel left out or for your outlook to be affected."
   - "Have you been in this situation before? What did you do to cope?"
   - "What can we take away from that experience to compensate for distance from the team?
   - "If there are special resources we need to purchase, let me know so we can discuss them."

4. Revisit the plan
   - "Let's get back together so I can hear from you about how things are going. When is a good time for you in the next two weeks?"

When Pat was finished, Keri complimented Pat's worksheet.

"This is going so well, I think we should keep going," said Keri. "Is that okay with you?"

"Sure," Pat replied. "Let's address Jack's situation next."

"Okay. If I recall correctly, Jack is getting ready to retire in three years and you think that's affecting his performance. You might be right about the cause, but tell me about the lack of performance again."

Pat sighed and said, "Although Jack is meeting expectations, I think he's coasting. Based on his experience, knowledge, and abilities, he could be doing more. Actually, he should be doing more considering his past performance. Besides that, I need him to set a good example because some team members look up to him."

"You're right," answered Keri. "That is a problem and the coaching opportunity it falls under is Motivation. Here are the steps. Let me know if you need any help when filling out the worksheet."

Coaching Opportunity: Motivation

Provide motivation when someone is meeting expectations, but could do better based on his/her education, experience, and ability.

	Model Steps	Motivation Steps
Before Coaching	1. Evaluate the situation	a. Observe behavior and/or result
		b. Match the situation with one of the five opportunities (see page 47)
		c. Take notes on how you will approach the situation using the remaining steps as a guideline
Coaching	2. Describe the situation	a. Describe what you've seen/heard
		b. Discuss the impact
		c. Gain agreement that the employee could do better
	3. Plan a change	a. Explore ideas that will help the employee meet his/her potential:
		• Would the employee take on new tasks and responsibilities?
		• Would the employee serve as a role model for other team members?
		• Encourage team member to participate fully
		b. Review ideas and get commitment
		c. Express enthusiasm for positive impacts to the team
	4. Revisit the plan	a. Set a date
		b. Be supportive

Coaching Worksheet – How would you coach Jack?

1. Evaluate the situation

2. Describe the situation

3. Plan a change

4. Revisit the plan

Coaching Worksheet Example – Possible Coaching Results for Jack

1. Evaluate the situation
   - He does quality work and is meeting job requirements (minimum expectations). However, with his experience (24 years in this field), he should be more productive (he was in the past).
   - He's retiring in three years. This may not have anything to do with Jack's change in performance, but it may.

2. Describe the situation
   - "Jack, I want to talk to you about how we can improve team performance."
   - "Our team is not meeting some of our key goals. While you're meeting expectations of the job, you could do so much more. I need every team member contributing 100%."
   - "If every team member doesn't work at the level of their abilities, we'll continue to let our customers down and not meet two of our core values: results and stewardship."
   - "What are your thoughts on this matter?"

3. Plan a change
   - "Is there something I could do to make the work environment more appealing?"
   - There could be something within your power, but don't stop here. Optimally, employees need to find internal motivation.
   - "I need someone to lead implementation of the new online processing function; is that something that interests you?" OR "Would you set the bar for the new online processing function?" OR "Would you train the others in the new online processing function?"
   - "Okay, it looks like we've agreed to…"

4. Revisit the plan
   - "Let's get back together so I can hear from you about how things are going. When is a good time for you in the next two weeks?"
   - "Let me know if you need anything."

Keri read Pat's worksheet and remarked, "Motivation is a huge topic, so it's hard to do it justice in just a page of coaching notes. However, you did a nice job of concisely capturing the essence of coaching someone like Jack. The fact that you're quite a bit younger is another justification for taking a coaching approach. You're more likely to have success than if you just told him to get his rear in gear, so to speak. Okay, who's next?" Keri asked.

"That would be Dr. Jekyll, who is also known as Jerry," Pat said dryly.

Keri chuckled and said, "Okay, I get it, but I actually think your beef is with Mr. Hyde."

Pat laughed out loud. "Ha! That's true! He transformed into another person altogether. On probation, he consistently delivered quality work on time. After probation, he's consistently late with poor-quality work."

"What was the opportunity you put Jerry in?"

"I put him down for Alignment."

"Great. You know the drill by now. Go ahead and fill out a coaching worksheet for Jerry and we'll take a look at it together."

Coaching Opportunity: Alignment

Provide alignment when someone doesn't meet expectations from time to time.

	Model Steps		Alignment Steps
Before Coaching	1. Evaluate the situation	a.	Observe behavior and/or result
		b.	Match the situation with one of the five opportunities (see page 47)
		c.	Take notes on how you will approach the situation using the remaining steps as a guideline
Coaching	2. Describe the situation	a.	Introduce the situation without putting the person on the defensive
		b.	Discuss the impact
		c.	Gain agreement that there is room for development
	3. Plan a change	a.	Collaborate on a change by asking one or all of the following:
			• What is getting in the way of consistency?
			• What ideas do you have for improving consistency?
			• What can be done to address the lapse in performance?
			• I have a suggestion. May I share it?
		b.	Review discussion and get commitment
			• So it sounds like, I will...and you will...Is that your understanding?
	4. Revisit the plan	a.	Set a date
		b.	Be supportive

Coaching Worksheet — How would you coach Jerry?

1. Evaluate the situation

2. Describe the situation

3. Plan a change

4. Revisit the plan

Coaching Worksheet Example – Possible Coaching Results for Jerry

1. Evaluate the situation
   - He's consistently late with work that is poor in quality.
   - He knows how to do the work; he was consistently on time with quality work while on probation.
   - Could he be bored already? He's been here only 14 months, but maybe he's not being challenged enough.
   - When someone is consistently late, realignment (a more directive approach) is better. However, this is the first time I've approached Jerry about this issue. Alignment is a better approach with which to begin.
   - Have I recognized his accomplishments?

2. Describe the situation
   - "Jerry, I want to talk to you about providing services to our customers."
   - "I've noticed a drop in the quantity and quality of your work in the last month. Specifically, the on-time rate dropped 60% and the error rate increased 22%."
   - "What are some of the implications for our customers?"

3. Plan a change
   - "What ideas do you have for improving the situation?"
   - "That sounds like a good start. Any other ideas?"
   - "So, it looks like we've agreed to...Is that your understanding?"

4. Revisit the plan
   - "Let's get back together so I can hear from you how things are going. When is a good time for you in the next two weeks?"
   - "Let me know if you need anything."

"I think Jerry has a lot of potential," Keri told Pat after she read Jerry's coaching worksheet. "I really hope you can get him back on track. By the way, didn't you have two employees who fit in Alignment?"

"Yes," Pat answered dejectedly. "This is one of my bigger challenges so far."

"It can't be that bad," said Keri.

"It's pretty bad," said Pat. "Don shows a lack of respect for me in body language and words. I saw him roll his eyes at another employee when I was talking during a staff meeting. Eye contact is much less than any other person on the team. He criticizes my ideas in front of others. I understand that people should feel comfortable to challenge me, but until recently he has never supported one of my ideas. He has made some improvement, but he still calls me 'kid' and has a superior tone as he explains 'the way we've always done it.'"

"Well, let's get to work on Don's worksheet and see if we can't get this thing worked out."

Coaching Worksheet — How would you coach Don?

1. Evaluate the situation

2. Describe the situation

3. Plan a change

4. Revisit the plan

Coaching Worksheet Example — Possible Coaching Results for Don

1. Evaluate the situation
   - Don shows a lack of respect for me. I saw him roll his eyes at another employee when I was talking. He criticizes my ideas in front of others. I understand that people should feel comfortable to challenge me, but until recently he has never supported one of my ideas.
   - There is some progress: he's making more eye contact with me during staff and one-on-one meetings; he smiled at me when I made a suggestion the other day.
   - Have I acknowledged his experience and recognized his accomplishments?

2. Describe the situation
   - "I want to talk to you about improving our working relationship."
   - "I've noticed signs that you don't respect me as a supervisor. Your words and body language show a lack of respect (provide instances from above)."
   - "Not only does this affect our relationship, what do you think this does to the team?"
   - "So it sounds like you agree that this is something that should be addressed."

3. Plan a change
   - "Is there something I can do to earn your respect?"
   - "I'm glad to hear that you've seen growth in me over the last three months."
   - "What ideas do you have to improve your attitude toward me?"
   - "So, I will…and you will…Is that your understanding?"

4. Revisit the plan
   - "Let's get back together so we can check progress. When is a good time for you in the next two weeks?"
   - "I appreciate your cooperation."

After reviewing Don's coaching worksheet together, Keri commented on Pat's work. "Nice job on your coaching notes for Don. A coaching session or two like that and Don's respect will be taken up a notch. Coaching doesn't work for all people or all situations. However, based on Don's growing respect for you during Jobs 1 and 2, he's ready to respond to your coaching."

"Thanks for the positive feedback. It's really helpful and nice," Pat said genuinely, "but I'm pretty nervous about this next one. When you say that coaching doesn't work for everyone, I'm really not sure it's going to work on Lorraine the…"

"Pain, right?" Keri interrupted. "Go ahead and tell me about Lorraine again."

"Well, she is a difficult person. There's not a day that goes by when she doesn't make a rude remark or try to put someone down. Her level of productivity is fine, but if her behavior is ignored, more and more team members will resist working with her. Everyone except John and Meredith has threatened to quit working with her."

"Wow. That's definitely a situation you need to get under control," said Keri. "That can really affect the morale of the team, especially if allowed to fester."

"Well, now that I'm so much more comfortable with this process, I'm looking forward to addressing these issues with a coherent plan."

"Sounds good," said Keri. "Go ahead and fill out the worksheet and we can discuss what you come up with."

Coaching Opportunity: Realignment

Provide realignment when someone consistently isn't meeting expectations.

<table>
<tr><td></td><td>Model Steps</td><td colspan="2">Realignment Steps</td></tr>
<tr><td rowspan="3">Before Coaching</td><td>1. Evaluate the situation</td><td>a.</td><td>Observe behavior and/or result</td></tr>
<tr><td></td><td>b.</td><td>Match the situation with one of the five opportunities (see page 47)</td></tr>
<tr><td></td><td>c.</td><td>Take notes on how you will approach the situation using the remaining steps as a guideline</td></tr>
</table>

	Model Steps		Realignment Steps
Before Coaching	1. Evaluate the situation	a.	Observe behavior and/or result
		b.	Match the situation with one of the five opportunities (see page 47)
		c.	Take notes on how you will approach the situation using the remaining steps as a guideline
Coaching	2. Describe the situation	a.	Describe the behavior that is a problem
		b.	State the impact
		c.	Gain agreement that there is a problem
		d.	Express your concern
	3. Plan a change	a.	Work on a solution by asking one or all of the following:
			• What is getting in the way of your success?
			• What can be done to address the problem?
			• What will you do to deal with the problem?
		b.	If employee doesn't generate an acceptable solution, say "I have a suggestion...Is that acceptable?"
		c.	Review discussion and get commitment
			• So it sounds like, you will...Is that your understanding?
			• If no response or commitment, provide a plan of action
	4. Revisit the plan	a.	Set a date
		b.	Be supportive

Coaching Worksheet — How would you coach Lorraine?

1. Evaluate the situation

2. Describe the situation

3. Plan a change

4. Revisit the plan

Coaching Worksheet Example — Possible Coaching Results for Lorraine

1. Evaluate the situation
   - Lorraine is a difficult person. Lorraine is sarcastic and doesn't seem to respect anyone. Almost the entire staff refuses to work with her.
   - She doesn't exhibit these behaviors with me or her customers. It seems to be limited to her peers.
   - Have I given her praise when she does especially well?

2. Describe the situation
   - "Lorraine, I want to talk to you about an ongoing issue that affects team collaboration. We've talked before about signs of disrespect and difficult behaviors toward team members. I haven't seen sustained improvement in this area. Some of our team members are uncomfortable working with you."
   - "Your behavior is preventing the team from functioning as a unit." (Pause; let Lorraine respond.)
   - "I am concerned that you are not correcting your behavior."

3. Plan a change
   - "What can you do to address the problem?"
   - "That's a good start. What else can you do?"
   - "I also have two suggestions. First, write something positive about each person on the team and the value they bring to the team. Second, we need to meet on a weekly basis to review implementation of our ideas and check progress. Are these suggestions acceptable?"
   - "So, it sounds like you're going to…(review the items). Can you commit to this plan?"

4. Revisit the plan
   - "When is a good time for you to meet with me next week?"
   - "I am confident that you can be successful. Let me know if you need anything else."

"Well, this is a difficult one," Keri told Pat when she was finished, "but I think your coaching approach with Lorraine is very good. Of course, it's not going to be just a one-time coaching session—you will need many. Continue to meet for coaching and progress reports regularly. If Lorraine doesn't respond to your coaching, let me know."

"Does that mean you'll address it?" asked Pat.

"No. That's not my role. What it means is that we're not out of options when it comes to unchecked inappropriate behavior of an employee. We can consult Maria, our HR representative, for advice on next steps in the corrective discipline process. In the meantime, please be sure to document all of your performance discussions with Lorraine and Meredith. I hope it doesn't come to more serious measures, but we need good documentation just in case. Anytime you're redirecting employees, this is essential."

"Thanks for reminding me about Meredith," Pat said. "She's the other employee who needs realignment."

"Tell me what's going on with her," said Keri.

"Meredith's main issues are absenteeism and tardiness and, since I last spoke with her, she's continued to be late and excessively absent."

Keri's tone was cautious as she responded. "To help Meredith, you really need to be prepared. I'd like you to do a coaching worksheet as we've been doing already. Also, if you feel it's appropriate during the coaching, share this EAP (Employee Assistance Program) brochure with her. To minimize any potential discomfort for her, explain that nearly everyone uses this benefit at least once during their career. If you've ever used it, sharing that with her can go a long way in minimizing discomfort and building trust between the two of you."

Coaching Worksheet — How would you coach Meredith?

1. Evaluate the situation

2. Describe the situation

3. Plan a change

4. Revisit the plan

Coaching Worksheet Example – Possible Coaching Results for Meredith

1. Evaluate the situation
   - Meredith has issues with absenteeism and tardiness.
     - Absent – She has called in sick five days in the last three months (exceeds personal absence allotment for the quarter).
     - Tardy – She has been late six times (ranging from 15 to 30 minutes) in the last three months.
   - We've talked before and she disclosed some of her personal/family problems. I feel sorry for her, but I can't ignore these issues.
   - When she is here, she does fine. Have I commended her good work?

2. Describe the situation
   - "Meredith, I want to talk to you about your ongoing issues with absenteeism and tardiness. Since our last discussion, you have been late three more times and absent two more days. This exceeds your personal absence time."
   - "This situation is affecting the team's ability to serve our customers in a timely fashion. On two related occasions we failed to meet our service level agreement." (Pause; let Meredith respond.)
   - "I am concerned that you are not correcting this disruptive behavior."

3. Plan a change
   - "What can you do to address the situation?"
   - "You suggested that last time. What other ideas do you have?"
   - "May I make two suggestions? (Pause for a response.) Have you considered job sharing with Staci? Also, please read this EAP brochure. I have used the program's services and can tell you that it's professional and confidential."
   - "So, it sounds like you're going to...(review the items). Can you commit to this plan?"

4. Revisit the plan
   - "When is a good time for you to meet with me next week?"
   - "If you follow through with this plan, I am confident that you can be successful. Let me know if you need anything else."

"Great work on this last worksheet as well, Pat," Keri said as she handed back the one filled out for Meredith. "I think you're now prepared for one of the most common performance issues in the workplace. As is necessary, you're holding her accountable and treating her with respect at the same time. That's the magic of good coaching."

"Thanks Keri!" Pat was pretty happy with herself too. "Having a proven coaching model to guide me makes a big difference—I feel much more confident. Of course, having a personal coach like you is priceless."

"Well, you're welcome, and thanks for not just giving up like a lot of managers do. Anything else we should talk about?"

"Actually, there's one more we haven't addressed. Remember John, who accused me of favoritism?" Pat asked.

"Oops, I forgot. I think I suggested that his situation called for feedback rather than coaching. Is that right?"

Pat answered, "Yes. I wanted to address it right away, but I wasn't aware of the coaching approach at the time, so I simply talked to him about it."

Keri said, "I think you made the right decision and, so far, it's worked out. To me, here are the differences between coaching and feedback:

- All coaching is feedback, but not all feedback is coaching.

- Feedback is an attempt to address an issue, but coaching is a process for developing people.

- Coaching is a prolonged process of changing behavior (ranging from three to eight sessions on average), but feedback is usually a one or two-time event.

- Sometimes I start off with feedback and discover that coaching is also needed.

"I've got more paper to give you," Keri said apologetically. "This time it's a pair of pneumonic devices about giving and receiving feedback called POISE and PAUSE. I've also included an example of how POISE works."

Giving and Receiving Feedback

The steps below for giving and receiving feedback give you POISE and PAUSE, which are essential for effective communication of issues. Learning both methods promotes solid communication about mutual concerns.

Giving – How to give feedback (POISE for confidence to deliver feedback)

1. Purpose	State your purpose (to improve a situation).
2. Observed	State what you have seen (use "I statement").
3. Impact	State the potential impact (use "I statement").
4. Situation	Attack the situation, not the person.
5. Evaluate	Set a date to follow up and evaluate progress.

Receiving – How to receive feedback (PAUSE before responding)

1. Protect	Don't protect yourself; don't be defensive.
2. Active	Actively listen.
3. Understand	Understand and acknowledge concerns.
4. Situation	Attack the situation, not the person.
5. Evaluate	Suggest a date to follow up and evaluate progress.

Prepare for POISE Worksheet Example

POISE preparation is important when you need to give someone feedback. Use the questions below to plan your approach.

1. Purpose - What will you say to express your positive purpose?

(In a conference room) "John, as I said yesterday when I set up this meeting, I want to talk to you about improving our working relationship."

2. Observed - What will you say to state your observations in such a way that minimizes defensiveness? (Don't begin with "you.")

"I was surprised when I heard you say that I showed favoritism. Tell me about why you feel this way."

"John, would you like to hear my side of the story?"

3. Impact - What will you say to state the impact in such a way that promotes problem solving? (Don't begin with "you.")

"Would you agree that showing favoritism tears down trust and hurts team unity? It's something that must be resolved, isn't it?"

4. Situation - What will you say to ask for solutions and consider options?

"I have an idea about how this problem can be resolved, but I'd like to hear your thoughts first."

5. Evaluate - What will you say to set a date and evaluate progress?

"Although we've resolved this problem, I'd like to follow up with you to see how things are going with our resolution. Would next Tuesday at 4:00 work for you?"

Once they were finished reviewing the documents, Keri said to Pat: "I hope you find these two feedback processes helpful. The best way to get used to giving and receiving feedback this way is to actually try it out. After a while, you'll be more inclined to use coaching and feedback naturally and habitually. Remember, though, like coaching, feedback is best when you're prepared. Be sure to use the Feedback Worksheet in Appendix B."

Pat's eyes shone brightly as she told Keri, "Keri, you have been a wonderful coach. I remember that day I first came to your office. I was disconsolate then, but now I'm confident and seeing a whole world of possibilities. Thank you so much!"

Keri smiled broadly and said, "Well, you've been very coachable and easy to work with. It's so refreshing to find a supervisor who is willing to listen and learn. Your openness and candidness are among your best qualities. With all of your good qualities and your application of the techniques we've discussed and practiced over the past few months, you are on the road to success. I'd wish you the best, but that sounds final. My door is always open for you."

Appendix A

Coaching Opportunity: OJT (On-the-job Training)

Provide OJT when someone doesn't have a job skill. Use this job aid for providing OJT, especially if you delegate the task.

Model Steps	OJT Steps
1. Evaluate	
	a. Determine if OJT is needed
2. Describe the situation	a. Prepare the Learner
	b. Establish a positive atmosphere; empathize with the learner
	c. Provide background; help the learner understand the purpose and benefit; explain what happens when done incorrectly
	d. Provide resources (equipment, materials, etc.)
3. Plan a change	a. Demonstrate the process using SMART

S = Start: explain when this task needs to be started
M = Materials: go over the materials needed to perform this task
A = Actions: demonstrate the task by carefully going over the steps
R = Result: show the result and how it meets the task standard
T = Task standard: how the employee will know it was done as expected

b. Encourage questions; make sure questions are answered

c. Have the learner perform the task

d. Offer support and guidance

e. Provide corrections as needed

f. When the required performance is observed, reinforce it

g. Continue until the employee can perform consistently with your help

4. Revisit the plan

a. Establish a plan for follow-up

b. Check back later for questions; evaluate progress

c. When employee can do it consistently without your help, congratulate him/her on mastering the skill

d. Determine whether OJT accomplished the goal

Appendix B

Prepare for POISE Worksheet

Preparation is important when you need to give someone feedback. Use the questions below to plan your approach.

1. Purpose

   What will you say to express your positive purpose?

2. Observed

   What will you say to state your observations in such a way that minimizes defensiveness? (Don't begin with "you.")

3. Impact

   What will you say to state the impact in such a way that promotes problem solving? (Don't begin with "you.")

4. Situation

   What will you say to ask for solutions and consider options?

5. Evaluate

   What will you say to set a date and evaluate progress?

Appendix C

Performance Appraisal Form

Employee name: _____

Job Title: _____

Job Description:

Five Key Accomplishments:

Three Strengths:

Two Areas of Improvement or Development:

Summary of performance:

Rating: ☐ Exceeds   ☐ Meets   ☐ Improvement needed

Appendix D

Job Aid: Situational Coaching Model

Steps   Opportunities

Before Coaching

1. Evaluate the situation
   - Observe behavior and/or result
   - Match the situation with one of the five opportunities (see page 47)
   - Take notes on how you will approach the situation using the remaining steps as a guideline

Coaching

2. Describe the situation
   - Introduce the opportunity
   - Discuss the impact
   - Gain agreement that there is a situation that needs to be addressed

3. Plan a change
   - Collaborate on a solution
   - Ensure understanding
   - Gain commitment

4. Revisit the plan
   - Set a date
   - Be supportive

Opportunities:
- OJT
- Encouragement
- Motivation
- Alignment
- Realignment

Appendix E

Job Aid: Coaching Worksheet

1. Evaluate the situation

2. Describe the situation

3. Plan a change

4. Revisit the plan